the everyman series

being God's man...
by walking a new path

Real Men. Real Life. Powerful Truth.

Stephen Arterburn

Kenny Luck & Todd Wendorff

WATERBROOK
PRESS

BEING GOD'S MAN...BY WALKING A NEW PATH

All Scripture quotations, unless otherwise indicated, are taken from the *Holy Bible, New International Version®. NIV®*. Copyright © 1973, 1978, 1984 by International Bible Society. Used by permission of Zondervan Publishing House. All rights reserved. Scripture quotations marked (NASB) are taken from the *New American Standard Bible®*. (NASB). © Copyright The Lockman Foundation 1960, 1962, 1963, 1968, 1971, 1972, 1973, 1975, 1977, 1995. Used by permission. (www.Lockman.org).

Trade Paperback ISBN 978-1-57856-919-9
eBook ISBN 978-0-307-55176-4

Copyright © 2004 by Kenny Luck and Todd Wendorff

Published in association with the literary agency of Alive Communications, Inc., 7680 Goddard Street, Suite 200, Colorado Springs, CO 80920.

Published in the United States by WaterBrook, an imprint of the Crown Publishing Group, a division of Penguin Random House LLC, New York.

WATERBROOK® and its deer colophon are registered trademarks of Penguin Random House LLC.

146122990

contents

welcome to the every man
Bible study series

As Christian men, we crave true-to-life, honest, and revealing Bible study curricula that will equip us for the battles that rage in our lives. We are looking for resources that will get us into our Bibles in the context of mutually accountable relationships with other men. But like superheroes who wear masks and work hard to conceal their true identities, most of us find ourselves isolated and working alone on the major issues we face. Many of us present a carefully designed public self while hiding our private self from view. This is not God's plan for us.

Let's face it. We all have trouble being honest with ourselves, particularly in front of other men.

As developers of a men's ministry, we believe that many of the problems among Christian men today are direct consequences of an inability to practice biblical openness—being honest about our struggles, questions, and temptations—and to connect with one another. Our external lives may be in order, but storms of unprocessed conflict, loss, and fear are eroding our resolve to maintain integrity. Sadly, hurting Christian men are flocking to unhealthy avenues of relief instead of turning to God's Word and to one another.

We believe the solution to this problem lies in creating opportunities for meaningful relationships among men. That's why we designed this Bible study series to be thoroughly interactive. When a man practices biblical openness with other men, he moves from secrecy to candor, from isolation to connection, and from pretense to authenticity.

Kenny and Todd developed the study sessions at Saddleback Church in Lake Forest, California, and at King's Harbor Church in Redondo Beach, California, where they teach men's Bible studies. At these studies, men hear an outline of the Bible passage, read the verses together, and then answer a group discussion question at their small-group tables. The teaching pastor then facilitates further discussion within the larger group.

This approach is a huge success for many reasons, but the key is that, deep down, men really do want close friendships with other guys. We don't enjoy living on the barren islands of our own secret struggles. However, many men choose to process life, relationships, and pressures individually because they fear the vulnerability required in small-group gatherings. *Suppose someone sees behind my carefully constructed image? Suppose I encounter rejection after revealing one of my worst sins?* Men willingly take risks in business and the stock market, sports and recreation, but we do not easily risk our inner lives.

Many church ministries are now helping men win this battle, providing them with opportunities to experience Christian male companionship centered in God's Word. This study series aims to supplement and expand that good work around the country. If these lessons successfully reach you, then they will also reach every relationship and domain that you influence. That is our heartfelt prayer for every man in your group.

how to use this study guide

As you prepare for each session, first review the **Key Verse** and **Goals for Growth,** which reveal the focus of the study at hand. Discuss as a group whether or not you will commit to memorizing the Key Verse for each session. The **Head Start** section then explains why these goals are necessary and worthwhile. Each member of your small group should complete the **Connect with the Word** section *before* the small-group sessions. Consider this section to be your personal Bible study for the week. This will ensure that everyone has spent some time interacting with the biblical texts for that session and is prepared to share responses and personal applications. (You may want to mark or highlight any questions that were difficult or particularly meaningful so you can focus on those during the group discussion.)

When you gather in your small group, you'll begin by reading aloud the **Head Start** section to remind everyone of the focus for the current session. The leader will then invite the group to share any questions, concerns, insights, or comments arising from their personal Bible study during the past week. If your group is large, consider breaking into subgroups of three or four people (no more than six) at this time.

Next, get into **Connect with the Group,** starting with the **Group Opener.** These openers are designed to get at the heart of each week's lesson. They focus on how the men in your group relate to the passage and topic you are about to discuss. The group leader will read aloud the opener for that week's session and then facilitate interaction on the **Discussion Questions** that follow. (Remember: Not everyone has to offer an answer for every question.)

Leave time after your discussion to complete the **Standing Strong** exercises, which challenge each man to consider, *What's my next move?* As you openly express your thoughts to the group, you'll be able to hold one another accountable to reach for your goals.

Finally, close in **prayer**, either in your subgroups or in the larger group. You may want to use this time to reflect on and respond to what God has done in your group during the session. Also invite group members to share their personal joys and concerns, and use this as "grist" for your prayer time together.

By way of review, each lesson is divided into the following sections:

To be read or completed *before* the small-group session:
- **Key Verse**
- **Goals for Growth**
- **Head Start**
- **Connect with the Word** (home Bible study: 30-40 minutes)

To be completed *during* the small-group session:
- Read aloud the **Head Start** section (5 minutes)
- Discuss personal reaction to **Connect with the Word** (10 minutes)
- **Connect with the Group** (includes the **Group Opener** and discussion of the heart of the lesson: 30-40 minutes)
- **Standing Strong** (includes having one person pray for the group; challenges each man to take action: 20 minutes)

rogue warriors for God

Who will you become?

Will you discover your true reason for living, enter the battle, and become a new man in Christ? Or will you settle for less than God's desire for you? That's your decision. No one can make it for you. However, to become more like Christ, you will have to embrace a new way of living.

This kind of can-do attitude is what the Navy SEALs look for in a man. In many ways SEALs are rogue warriors. Totally unconventional. Guys who will do anything to win the battle. Though the word *rogue* actually means "vagrant," "scoundrel," and "tramp," these larger-than-life men have given it a new and proud meaning.

SEALs live by a different code that is guided by a set of unwavering commitments, such as:

- I will totally commit to what I believe, and I will risk all that I have for these beliefs.
- I will always make it crystal clear where I stand and what I believe.
- I will always be easy to find; I'll be at the center of the battle.

Living by such a code requires men who won't shrink from the battle. One such man is Richard Marcinko, former Navy SEAL, special ops expert, and author of the Rogue Warrior series of action-adventure novels. This is what his Web site says about him:

Richard is one of the nation's most accomplished and recognized special operations experts, with over 30 years of experience in a variety of specialties including counter-terrorism, intelligence and special operations. After enlisting in the Navy, Marcinko worked his way up to the rank of captain. He was the first commanding officer and founder of two of the military's premier counter-terrorist units: SEAL TEAM SIX and Red Cell. The legendary SEAL TEAM SIX engaged in highly classified missions from Central America to the Middle East, the North Sea to Africa and beyond. Commanding Red Cell, Marcinko was directed to use his team to test the Navy's antiterrorist capabilities. The result: he was able to infiltrate seemingly impenetrable, highly secured bases, nuclear submarines, ships, and other purported "secure areas."[1]

The apostle Paul wasn't a military man like Marcinko, but in spirit he was a rogue warrior for God. He was tough and uncompromising. He held to a code that defined his life. He lived on purpose, not by accident.

---

1. Biographical information on Richard Marcinko found at the Simon and Schuster Web site, www.simonsays.com/content/content.cfm?sid=33& pid=360302&agid=13.

If you choose to become this kind of man, made new and unwilling to compromise, then let this great apostle lead the way. In 1 Corinthians 4:16, Paul said, "Therefore I urge you to imitate me." Will you do it?

Before landing in a Jerusalem jail and being sent to Rome to live out his final years under house arrest, Paul wrote an epistle to the believers in Rome. This letter was his finest work, a compilation of everything he understood about the gospel, the living message of Christ's saving power that was heralded across the Roman Empire. It was the only message that could bring about lasting change in men's hearts.

Paul was well aware that the men in Rome needed to be set free from their sinful lifestyles. After all, Rome was a city for men. From athletics to war, Roman culture represented all that a thoroughly secular man stood for. It reeked with sin and debauchery. Any and all fantasies were joyfully indulged in Rome. Men consumed with their fleshly desires crowded the streets.

Even so, many men in the city converted to Christianity, and their lives were radically changed. Now, as followers of Christ, they were captivated by a new calling in life. Having been made new through the gospel message, these men now wanted to live out that gospel in their city and impact others. Paul challenged every man to take up that new calling—without losing the desire for adventure and risk.

As we explore the first eleven chapters of Romans in this study, we will see how the gospel message not only saves us but also sanctifies us, transforming us from within.[2] Many men today find it easy to

---

2. An exploration of the final chapters of Romans can be found in the study titled *Being God's Man...by Claiming Your Freedom*.

believe that Christ has the power to save them, yet they often have difficulty seeing how He is able to make them completely new. So a struggle rages within, and we wonder, *How will I ever experience lasting change within my heart and soul? I'm saved, but am I becoming a different person?*

Our goal in this study is to stimulate personal reflection and honest dialogue with God and with other men about the power Christ unleashes in our lives. As you work through each session, look in the mirror at your own life and ask yourself some hard questions. Whether you are doing this study individually or in a group, realize that being completely honest with yourself, with God, and with others will produce the greatest growth.

Our prayer is that through the gospel message, your life will be radically changed, and that you, like Paul, will become a rogue warrior for God, living out your new identity in Christ in total freedom.

a new you

Key Verses

Through him and for his name's sake, we received grace and apostleship to call people from among all the Gentiles to the obedience that comes from faith. And you also are among those who are called to belong to Jesus Christ. (Romans 1:5-6)

Goals for Growth

- Allow God to give me a new core identity.
- Be open to a new mission and purpose for my life.
- See the ways I have been made new in Christ.

Head Start

Years ago a television commercial announced: "A man is what a man does." Do you agree?

It's certainly true that most men see themselves through the lens of what they do. Their occupation often determines their core identity. Whether you are a doctor, a lawyer, a plumber, or a restaurant manager, it is difficult to find complete satisfaction in your work. That's just the way it is. God never designed us to be fully content in what we do. Instead, He wants us to find contentment in who we are in Him. Yet it's rare to find a man whose identity is wrapped around what God says about him.

God's view of us is more important than what we do, and it's the truth. Nevertheless, men struggle to hear God's voice in the midst of all the static life produces. They're busy trying to become somebody, often without any input at all from God. What often results is that men feel they haven't reached their full potential.

Paul wrote the book of Romans to show us how Christ sets us free from a deluded view of self. No longer held back by a wrong view of self, we are released to reach our full potential in Christ. It all starts with taking on a new core identity, which changes the way we see ourselves now and points the way to who we will become in the future.

In the movie *Sommersby*, Jack Sommersby returns home at the end of the Civil War to a farm in ruins and a wife who wishes he were dead. Jack is no longer the same person he was six years earlier when he left home—a gambling, wife-beating drunkard. He's become a totally different person who is generous and caring toward others. The difference astounds the suspicious townspeople who wonder whether this new Jack is really the old Jack they've always known.

The apostle Paul likewise became a completely different person. He had been a religious Jew all his life, a zealous crusader dedicated to wiping out any threat to Judaism. Feared by all who lived in Palestine during the first century, Paul had imprisoned, beaten, and even killed Christians. Then he met Jesus on the road to Damascus, and he was changed forever. Paul was truly a man transformed from the inside out. Jesus had changed his core identity and had given him a new purpose for living.

Yet people didn't believe it. They still feared him. It must have taken courage for Ananias to lay his hands on Saul, who would become Paul, and proclaim: "This really is a new Saul!" (See Acts 9:17.) For us, the message is clear: if a man is to live differently, he must first see himself as a new man in Christ.

Connect with the Word

Read Romans 1:1-13.

1. What words and phrases did Paul use in verse 1 to describe his core identity?

2. Imagine viewing yourself as a servant of Christ. What would be some of the practical implications for you?

3. In verse 5, Paul is saying that faith produces obedience, but how is obedience a prerequisite for living out your new identity by faith? In what ways has your belief in your new identity been reinforced by the steps of obedience you've taken?

4. Paul was determined to visit the believers in Rome to encourage them in their faith (verses 11-13). What does his selfless act reveal about the work of Christ in the heart of a man? How is this possible only through a changed identity?

5. In what ways does Paul help you see that you were created for a greater purpose than just living for yourself?

Connect with the Group

Group Opener
Discuss the group-opener question and the discussion questions that follow.
(Suggestion: As you begin your group discussion time in each of the following sessions, consider forming smaller groups of three to six men. This will allow more time for discussion and give everyone an opportunity to share their thoughts and struggles.)

Consider the statement that appeared at the beginning of Head Start: "A man is what a man does." Do you agree or disagree with this statement? Explain.

Discussion Questions
a. Who are you? (*Suggestion:* Share with the other guys how you see yourself, and ask them, "Who do you see when you look at me?")

b. In what ways does God enable us to see ourselves differently so that we can live a new life in Him?

c. Paul was clear about his new identity in Christ. How might you view yourself differently after studying this passage? (*Hint:* See Romans 1:1,5.)

d. What is your greatest fear or struggle with owning your new identity in Christ?

e. Share with the group your response to the final question in Connect with the Word.

f. What would it look like in your group if the guys "mutually encouraged" one another regularly (verse 12)? What could it mean for your group specifically?

Standing Strong

How do you tend to see yourself in the following areas? (Be as honest and revealing as you can.)

work

family

strengths and weaknesses

interests

education

Now go back to each category and ask yourself: In what ways might the truths I've learned about my new identity in Christ change my perspective in each category? Pray with another man in the group, asking God to give you this new view of your core identity.

faith walk

Key Verses

I am not ashamed of the gospel, because it is the power of God for the salvation of everyone who believes: first for the Jew, then for the Gentile. For in the gospel a righteousness from God is revealed, a righteousness that is by faith from first to last, just as it is written: "The righteous will live by faith." (Romans 1:16-17)

Goals for Growth

- Understand that the gospel empowers me to a new life of faith in Christ.
- Give up trusting in my own efforts to be righteous.
- Embrace obedience to God as a new way of life.

Head Start

So much of a man's life is about hard work. He works for a living, works on his marriage, works at being a good dad, works on controlling his impulses. Men often believe it's up to them to make the necessary changes in their lives to bring about spiritual growth. Yet when a man muscles his way through life, he leaves no room for God's grace.

The apostle Paul wrote to the Roman believers to inspire them to live a new kind of life—a life of faith. Sheer willpower strikes out in this life; mere self-effort makes no headway. Instead, the "new" man walks the path of surrender and faithful obedience, believing that God has everything worked out. It's a matter of faith. But often we don't know what that looks like.

God wants you to live by faith in Him alone, trusting that He knows best. Is this your struggle? Are you holding back from giving God full control of your life? That's like a man who gets married and then calls home every day to ask his wife whether he's still hitched. Yes, you're married, so live like you are! Or it's like a man who is always stopping his car and making sure the engine isn't falling out. He'll never get anywhere. Just believe the engine's bolted down and keep driving! The man who lives in constant doubt is never able to fully enjoy his marriage or even the use of his car. Faith is required.

Where do we get this kind of faith? It's found in the gospel of Jesus Christ. The problem is, many of us have never taken our faith beyond salvation from God's judgment. We've been saved by faith and yet we're trying by our own efforts to make life work. But the Christian life is a walk of faith, and we need to learn to walk that walk.

Don't think for a minute that walking by faith means we check out and let God do all the work. That's not biblical faith. Philippians 2:12-13 reminds us that we "work out" what God "works in" us. It's a cooperative effort. Let God work in you, then you work that out by faith.

Troubled by a difficult boss? Let God work in you the qualities of patience and commitment to a good work ethic, no matter how you feel. Trust that God knows best and then work diligently and patiently out of respect for your boss.

Faith is the controlling factor in a new man's life. A man who responds in obedience truly believes God's way is best. The hard part of the whole deal is faith, not obedience. Obeying God may be difficult, but we will never obey Him if we do not trust Him.

Connect with the Word

Read Romans 1:14-17.

1. Why do you think Paul is obligated (a debtor), eager to preach, and unashamed of the gospel (verses 14-16)?

2. How is the power of God displayed in the gospel (verse 16)?

3. What happened in your life after you heard the gospel and were saved?

4. In verse 17, Paul tells us that God has given us His righteousness through faith in Christ. We are declared right with Him, and He no longer sees us as sinners. How does knowing this help you live your life in complete trust and obedience to Him?

5. In what ways is righteousness from God different from other kinds of goodness?

6. What does it look like for a righteous man to live by faith alone? What hinders us from doing so?

Connect with the Group

Group Opener
Read the group opener aloud and discuss the questions that follow.

Do you hold back from fully trusting God? Do you find it too difficult?

If I (Todd) were to extend a massive cable across the Grand Canyon and hook a pulley to it with a one-man harness seat, would you be willing to hop on? If you're the daring type who's always looking for adventure, then pulling yourself across this breathtaking chasm would be the rush of a lifetime. Let's assume that's the kind of man you are.

But what if, while extending the cable, I ran out of line and came up two feet short? Then, in order to complete the line, I spliced onto the end some brown twine. Would you joyfully launch yourself into the air now? Would it be a rush—or the stupidest thing you've ever done? Hey, it's only a few feet of twine; the rest is indestructible cable!

No?

As a follower of Christ, you can cling to a salvation that's far stronger than any cable. But are you holding back, splicing on a bit of twinelike self-effort? Just a couple feet of this kind of twine is enough to bring a good man down.

Discussion Questions
    a. In this session we have been talking about the lifelong process of sanctification, whereby the Holy Spirit works in a man's life to

make him more like Jesus, empowering God's man to walk by faith and obey God in everyday life. In your experience, is this process a continuous upward path, or is it typically two steps forward and one step back? Talk about it.

b. As you look back over your life, what evidence do you see that you are living more by faith, trusting God more?

c. What have you learned in this session that stands out to you as most important and personally relevant? Explain.

d. What steps can you take this week to begin eliminating some of the twine in your life?

Standing Strong

A "faith walk" requires a man to step out and completely trust that God will support him. In practical terms, what could this faith walk look like in your life during the coming week? the coming year?

the heart of darkness

Key Verses

As it is written: "There is no one righteous, not even one; there is no one who understands, no one who seeks God. All have turned away, they have together become worthless; there is no one who does good, not even one." (Romans 3:10-12)

Goals for Growth

- Become more aware of my own sinful human tendencies.
- Understand the destructive nature of sin in my life.
- Be willing to bring my sin before a holy and just God in true repentance.

Head Start

Ever seen the movie *Apocalypse Now*? Col. Walter E. Kurtz is an AWOL commander in the Vietnam War who's gone mad, raving mad. He's living in the heart of the Cambodian jungle, worshiped by natives as a sort of god. Thinking he is indeed God, Kurtz establishes his throne high up on a hill amid columns of human skulls. Capt. Benjamin L. Willard receives orders from headquarters to terminate the colonel "with extreme prejudice."

As I (Todd) watched this movie (with the famous line "I love the smell of napalm in the morning"), I wondered how a man could veer so far off course. How could a man with such training and expertise as Colonel Kurtz become such a lunatic? The answer is simple: sin.

The apostle Paul said that sin has caused the entire human race to veer off course. We have all veered off course. But do I include myself in that category? Well, maybe others are as crazy as Kurtz, but at least I'm a sane and functioning member of society. I couldn't be that bad.

But that's our problem. We think we're better than we really are. Each and every person who has ever lived on the face of the earth has sinned, grievously wounding the very heart of God. Look at what Genesis 6:5-6 says about us:

> The LORD saw how great man's wickedness on the earth had become, and that every inclination of the thoughts of his heart was only evil all the time. The LORD was grieved that he had made man on the earth, and his heart was filled with pain.

Ouch! Some of us know how evil our hearts are. Others have pretty well masked the truth with self-righteous activity. But the bottom line is that "all [are] under sin" (Romans 3:9). The apostle Paul spends the first three chapters of Romans dealing with the sinfulness of man's heart in order to prepare us to hear about the gift of God's

Son. We can't fully appreciate what God has done for us until we realize how far out of grace we've fallen. We will never experience the full benefit of grace until we see the darkness of sin in our hearts. A man can't be saved until he knows he's lost. Colonel Kurtz was lost and severely deluded, but he never admitted it.

Paul identified three types of lost men: the self-indulgent man, the self-righteous man, and the self-absorbed religious man. All three approaches to life are sinful and show us how much we need Christ. Can you relate? Have you ever been self-indulgent? Have you ever judged others while knowing you are no better than they? Have you ever put more emphasis on your own religious efforts than on your relationship with the Lord? This session will help you identify these trends in your life and make you more aware of why every man needs a Savior.

Connect with the Word

Read Romans 1:18–3:20.

The Self-Indulgent Sinner: Romans 1:18-32.

1. According to this passage, what has humankind done to distance itself from God's best? Why do you think men do these things?

2. How does this kind of behavior result in the sin of self-indulgence? According to Paul, what are the results of this kind of sin?

3. What are some of the idols we put in the place of God today? Which is most tempting to you? Explain.

The Self-Righteous Sinner: Romans 2:1-16.

4. What does it look like to judge another person (verses 1-2)?

5. Why do we pass judgment on others? How do stubbornness and unrepentance play into this tendency?

6. What did Paul say are the results of being self-righteous (verse 5)?

7. How have you seen the sin of self-righteousness displayed in your relationships with others?

The Self-Absorbed Religious Sinner: Romans 2:17–3:20.

8. What religious symbols did the self-righteous Jews hide behind? How about religious people in general?

9. What kind of religious activity do you do that's not heartfelt? How does it reveal sin in your life?

10. What's the problem with being a "religious" person?

11. How is Romans 3:9-20 a final judgment against all humankind?

Connect with the Group

Group Opener
Read the group opener aloud and discuss the questions that follow.

While talking with a friend recently, I (Todd) blasted a well-known Christian pastor who had fallen into a self-indulgent attitude that led to immorality. Even after being caught, he remained unrepentant and self-righteous, blaming his church for being unsupportive and defaming his character. He actually sued his own church after being fired!

I judged this man for his actions, called him a disgrace to the church, and held out no hope that he would ever recover. I felt good that I have held a higher moral standard than he. Yet, deeper within, I realize now that though this man was guilty as charged, so am I. My own sinfulness, past and present, reminds me why I need a Savior every second of every day.

Discussion Questions

a. How do you relate to this story? What does it show you about your own tendencies toward sin?

b. It is possible to acknowledge your sinfulness while knowing at the same time that you are infinitely beloved of God? Explain.

c. According to Paul, sin puts us on a slippery slope toward destruction. (See Romans 1:24-32.) When have you been most likely to slide down that hill in your own life?

d. According to Paul, what do the self-righteous do to make themselves look better than others? What is the danger in doing this? How do you fall into this trap?

e. Romans 3:9-20 describes the sinful tendencies found in a man. Which of these tendencies would you say is most prevalent in your life? How can you tell?

f. Paul closes this section by saying that we've all sinned, none of us seek God, and we are hopelessly lost in our sin. Why do you think we still struggle with secretly believing that there is some goodness in our hearts? How does this belief keep us from fully embracing the solution to our problem and living a new life?

Standing Strong

Describe how each of the following sins pervades your life:

self-indulgence

self-righteousness

self-religiosity

Pair up with another man and pray that a growing awareness of your own sin will prompt you to rely more on the Savior as you walk by faith.

help is on the way

Key Verses

Now a righteousness from God, apart from law, has been made known, to which the Law and the Prophets testify. This righteousness from God comes through faith in Jesus Christ to all who believe. (Romans 3:21-22)

Goals for Growth

- Become more grateful for all that Christ has done in my life.
- Abandon my own efforts at achieving righteousness.
- Become radically committed to true Christ-centered living.

Head Start

"I have good news and bad news," says the lawyer. "The bad news is that DNA testing shows your blood is all over the murder scene.... The good news is that your cholesterol is down to 130!"

When it's not part of a joke, good news can be a wonderful thing. But good news isn't really good until the bad news is really bad.

While driving through a neighborhood, my (Todd's) pastor friend Chris spotted a forest fire burning out of control. Realizing the fire was headed for a few isolated homes, he rushed from house to house to announce the bad news. It was the easiest thing he had ever done. Complete strangers listened closely to what he had to say: "I'm here to tell you there's a fire headed for your home."

That was all he had to say to get people up and out of their homes. They grabbed their pets and hurried to their cars. The bad news: their lives were in danger. The good news: they had been warned in enough time to evacuate.

Good news isn't good until the bad news is really bad. If Chris had said, "I think your fireplace is smoking," I doubt he would have seen the same immediate and committed response. The "badness" of the situation made the difference.

In the previous session, we examined the darkness of sin that lies within each of our hearts. We are deeply and hopelessly lost in sin. Left to our own devices, we're headed for eternal darkness, separated from our Creator God forever. (See Matthew 8:10-12.) We may harbor some secret pleasure deep within our hearts, make ourselves out to be better than we really are by putting others down, or fall short of a relationship with Christ by settling for meaningless religious activity. (See Romans 1:18–3:20.) Each of these responses points to sin in our lives.

The bad news is that we can't overcome sin by our own efforts. The good news is that God hasn't left us in sin; He has intervened in the darkness of our lives. All we need to do is receive what He has done on our behalf.

Conference speaker Steve Farrar says, "Looking within for the answer is like scuba diving in a cesspool." Did you get that? We're in a mess, and we will never see our way out. There is only one solution to our sin problem: Jesus Christ. What Jesus has done for us will mark us for the rest of our lives—and for eternity. Men made new by the gospel are made new by Christ alone. What He's done for us is nothing short of a miracle. It's not a leg up until we are back on our feet, nor is it a quick fix. It's the only fix.

Connect with the Word

Read Romans 3:21–5:21.

1. Define the following terms that describe the work of Christ in our lives. (*Suggestion:* Consult a Bible dictionary, a study Bible, or an online reference such as *www.blueletterbible.org* or *bible.crosswalk.com.*)

the righteousness of God

faith (belief)

grace

justification

sanctification

redemption

propitiation

glorification

Reflect on these words and their definitions in light of your hopeless situation as a sinner lost without Christ. What impact has knowing what Christ has done for you had on your relationship with Him?

2. Keeping in mind all that has been said about our sin and what Christ did to remove it, why do you think Paul raised the issue of boasting? (See Romans 3:27-28; 4:1-2.)

3. In light of Abraham's story, what do you think a life of faith looks like (4:1-24)? How does his example motivate you to live a life of faith?

4. Consider the obstacles to faith that Abraham faced in 4:18-21. What obstacles hinder our ability to live by faith in today's world? Which seem to hinder you the most?

5. Now that Christ has made us new, what should we be excited about (rejoice in)? (See Romans 5:2-3,11.)

6. Contrast the sin of Adam with the righteousness of Christ as well as the subsequent consequences of their actions (5:12-21). How does Christ's example motivate you to live a life of faith in Him alone?

Connect with the Group

Group Opener
Read the group opener aloud and discuss the questions that follow.

John once lived a life devoted to drugs, alcohol, and pornography. Only his love of surfing seemed to take the edge off his addictive lifestyle. He was a great surfer and knew all the surfing hot spots from Santa Barbara to the southern tip of Baja. Often he would head to Mexico with a van full of food, his surfboard, and skin-diving equipment and would camp out at some secret spot where he'd surf and dive for lobster. It seemed to John that life couldn't get any better—except for that nagging sin issue.

But in the years that followed, John found that surfing didn't give the same kick to his life, and he grew more and more discontented. His life had spun out of control, and his friends became concerned about him.

For some time, a few of John's surfing buddies had been talking to him about Christ, but he wasn't interested. Then when his life started unraveling, he began to listen and finally surrendered his heart to God.

John's life changed radically as he left his old lifestyle behind to serve the Lord. Old surfer friends would come up to him and say, "John, you've really changed. What happened to you?"

"It's my heart that's been changed," he'd answer.

Now John works for a union in the trade-show industry. His boss saw his potential and promoted him beyond his years and experience to a position as a trainer. John continues to find favor in his industry, even though he readily admits he isn't as qualified as others. We shouldn't be surprised—God graciously blesses and prospers the righteous.

Discussion Questions

a. Why do we sometimes think we can change on our own? What does John's story tell us about what Christ can do in a man's heart to bring about real life change?

b. Suppose you were a morally upright person before coming to Christ. Can you relate to John's story? If so, how?

c. When we realize what Christ has done to restore us to a right relationship with our heavenly Father, we realize the only right response is to cling to Him in utter dependence. Yet why do we struggle so much with the idea of being dependent upon others, including God? What is so difficult about showing that we are needy?

d. In what ways has your study of all that Christ has done for you made you a more grateful man? a man of deeper faith? a man more dependent on Christ?

e. When, if ever, have you resisted living a life of faith? Why?

f. What do you think it will take in a man's life today to replicate the life of faith Abraham lived? Brainstorm together, searching for practical applications.

Standing Strong

In light of the work of Christ, what steps will you take to live a life of faith like Abraham, who trusted God "in hope against hope" (Romans 4:18, NASB)?

choosing not to sin

Key Verses

We know that our old self was crucified with him so that the body of sin might be done away with, that we should no longer be slaves to sin—because anyone who has died has been freed from sin. (Romans 6:6-7)

Goals for Growth

- Determine to live free from the tyranny of sin.
- See myself as dead to sin and alive to God.
- Begin to make wise choices that lead to righteous living.

Head Start

Recently I (Todd) had a heart-piercing conversation with some close friends over dinner. My wife, Denise, had raised the question, "What are you trusting God for this year?"

After we went around the table, polling all four couples, my close friend David, a strong Christian man who runs a successful bond-trading office in downtown Chicago, said something that silenced the group: "If we say we have Christ in our lives, shouldn't we expect Him to change the way we act toward one another, especially toward our spouses and our kids? Shouldn't we be living in a way that's radically different from the people around us who don't know Christ?"

I responded, "Well, I guess you're right, David." I felt convicted that my own experience following Christ is somewhere between "totally defeated" and "radically changed."

Denise spoke up next. "Yes, but I give myself a lot more grace for the parts of me that are still in process." The others—Doug and Christine and Bryan and Belinda—agreed.

The discussion continued throughout the evening, and we ended by agreeing that if Christ has really changed us, our lives should show it. We know in theory how we should live, but how do we make it a daily reality?

I felt convicted and relieved at the same time. Denise was right, but so was David. Romans 5:20 tells us that where sin abounds, grace abounds all the more. When I sin, God covers me with His grace. But this should never be an excuse for living any way I please. Romans 6:1-2 sets me straight on that: "Shall we go on sinning so that grace may increase? By no means! We died to sin; how can we live in it any longer?"

So how can a man who is sinful and in need of God's grace consistently choose not to sin? The apostle Paul himself said that he was the chief of all sinners. (See 1 Timothy 1:15.) When he wrote this to young Timothy, was Paul looking back at the beginning of his life or was he referring to his current situation? If the latter, then how could Paul have admitted such a failure in his walk with Christ? Could he really have been as bad off as when he started? Did he not say to "put off [the] old self" and "put on the new self" (Ephesians 4:22,24)? Did he not say to "flee from youthful lusts" (2 Timothy 2:22, NASB)? Did he not say, "We are being renewed day by day" (2 Corinthians 4:16)?

Paul knew how sick his heart was, and yet in spite of this, he made tremendous progress in his Christian life. How is this possible? The answer lies in understanding the truth that in Christ we are now dead to sin, and then making choices consistent with that truth. We can still choose to sin anytime we like, but now we can also choose *not* to sin.

This could be the most perplexing truth in all the Scriptures. You are free to choose whether you will continue in your old sinful patterns of behavior or whether you will turn from continual, willful sin and live a new life. It's your choice.

As Paul said, we don't have to sin any longer—and we shouldn't want to either. Men made new are free to choose a new way of life. What will you choose?

Connect with the Word

Read Romans 6.

1. What did Paul mean when he said we should not continue sinning so that grace may abound (verses 1-2)? Did he mean that

our goal is sinless perfection? Where does the concept of spiritual maturity fit here?

2. What truths about your new condition as a believer do you find in verses 1-14?

3. If it is true that we are now dead to the control of sin in our lives (verse 6), what are we to do proactively to make that an everyday reality? (*Hint:* See verses 11-14.)

4. According to verse 16, what are the consequences of our sin? of our obedience?

5. What is the net effect of sin in our lives (verse 19)?

6. In verse 21, Paul asks a rhetorical question about the benefits of sin. Describe in your own words what you believe he is implying.

7. Would you say you are less motivated to sin because of what you've learned in verses 15-23? Explain. What principles are especially significant to you? Why?

Connect with the Group

Group Opener

Discuss the group-opener question and the discussion questions that follow.

Talk about the differences between sinless perfection and spiritual maturity in your Christian walk.

Discussion Questions

a. What seems to be the dilemma a Christian man faces when confronted with the truths of Romans 6?

b. How does Paul make it clear that a Christian man should not continue in a lifestyle of sin?

c. What is your honest response to the truth that you no longer have to choose sin? How has this motivated you to avoid significant temptation in the past?

d. Why do we continue to struggle with sinful behavior?

e. How is it helpful for us to know the true consequences of sin (Romans 6:15-23)? (*Note:* Notice how lawlessness—sin—leads to further lawlessness.)

f. What steps can you take this week to prevent sinful behavior? (Be as specific as possible.)

Standing Strong

According to Paul, what you believe about yourself is either true or false. How will what you believe about your new relationship to sin change the way you live as a man made new? In the space below, jot some specific changes you have noticed in yourself or would like to see in the future.

working harder, getting nowhere

Key Verse

I know that nothing good lives in me, that is, in my sinful nature. For I have the desire to do what is good, but I cannot carry it out. (Romans 7:18)

Goals for Growth

- Understand the utter futility of relying on the flesh to make me righteous.
- Realize that attempting to be more religious won't help me overcome sin.
- Become more dependent on Christ to help me in my daily struggle against sin.

Head Start

Some men are handy around the house; others aren't. I (Todd) am not. I've botched many a home-improvement project over the years.

And I've found that for an unhandy man like me, working harder rarely reaps the benefits I'm after.

I've learned a few things though. If it's rusted, don't tweak it. If it's the wrong tool, don't use it. If it's heavier than three times my body mass, don't try to lift it alone. Take it from me. After breaking all the rules, I eventually give up, frustrated, and call in a professional, getting myself further into debt than when I started. The frustrating part is that the harder I try, the worse the situation becomes. It's quite amazing how a leaky toilet can lead to a complete bathroom remodel!

Our efforts to conquer sin in our lives are like this. We've all tried on our own to conquer our sinful tendencies, and we've learned that it's harder than it looks. More often than not, we find ourselves right back where we started—or even worse off. On the other hand, once we realize how debilitating it is to struggle against sin through sheer willpower, we become motivated to learn the secret of living in freedom from it. To put it in home-improvement terms, I truly appreciate learning the right way to do a home-improvement project only after I've struggled to do it "my way" for a while.

In Romans 6 the apostle Paul answers the most nagging question we face: how do I walk free from a life of continual sin? Now in chapter 7 we seem to be right back where we started, struggling desperately to break free from a lifestyle of sin. Paul argues that the religious life he lived without Christ just put him deeper into a hole. (It's not until we read Romans 8 that Paul tells us how to break free from the sin that has a choke hold on us.)

Your old religious life apart from Christ has as much ability to keep you from a lifestyle of sin as an unhandy man has of doing a professional remodel. Someone once said, "The road to hell is paved with good intentions." That's Paul's point. Don't think for a minute that simply because you intend to live a better life, you will. In fact, the best intentions do not have the power to overcome the debilitating force of sin in your life. Working harder won't get you a better life.

The reality is we can't win this battle against sin without Christ and the power of the Holy Spirit, no matter how hard we try. Sin feeds on willpower and grows stronger through its nourishment. That's why Paul can say in Romans 7:19, "For what I do is not the good I want to do; no, the evil I do not want to do—this I keep on doing." He sounds schizophrenic. He's desperately wanting one thing but getting another. It's the same with us. Our struggle with the push and pull of sin is futile until we realize that victory is possible only with the help of the Holy Spirit (which we'll understand when we get to Romans 8). The fact is, until we find ourselves in complete desperation, we will never cry out for God to heal this wound within us.

Connect with the Word

Read Romans 7.

1. What is the connection between Paul's analogy of marriage and our relationship with the law (verses 1-6)?

2. How does knowing what is prohibited become a temptation for a man (verses 5,7-14)?

3. How does Paul describe the struggle we all encounter with sin (verses 15-23)?

4. What indications do you see in this passage that Christ does not seem to be effectively working in Paul's struggle?

5. What did Paul conclude about his condition apart from Christ's help (verses 24-25)?

6. To what extent can you relate to Paul's struggles? What area of temptation do you struggle with most? Explain.

Connect with the Group

Group Opener
Read the group opener aloud and discuss the questions that follow.

The rich young ruler in Luke 18 was a man who wanted to do something to fix his sin problem. He wanted desperately to inherit eternal life and be accepted by God, but he found little comfort in his religious activities or wealth. Neither had staying power in his life. Misguided, but desiring more, he approached Christ with the attitude, "If only I could do more, I'd be better than I am right now."

His efforts actually made things worse. The harder he tried and the more he did, the farther away he moved from his goal of righteousness.

Discussion Questions
a. Many men try to rectify their sin problem by working harder—and they end up farther away from their goal of holiness. When, if ever, has this been your experience? Explain.

b. Clearly, our fallen nature is not something we can transform. It must be replaced by a totally new nature—and only God can do that. What encouragement do you find in this truth? What do you find confusing or frustrating?

c. When you see a sign that says "Wet Paint," what is your first inclination? How does this relate to Romans 7:5,8?

d. According to Romans 7:5-6, as a Christian man you are joined no longer to the law, but to the Spirit. So when you try to conquer sin apart from Christ's help, what, in effect, are you doing? Why is this dangerous? (See Romans 7:15-23.)

e. The New American Standard version uses the word *flesh* four times to describe Paul's archenemy (Romans 7:5,14,18,25). How does our flesh mess up our progress toward victory over sin? In the most practical terms, what can we do to conquer the flesh?

Standing Strong

When have you seen your best intentions and efforts apart from Christ fail to help you in your battle with sin?

Choose to abandon all hope in self. Pray that God will prepare you for His solution to your sin problem—the Romans 8 solution.

you've got the power

Key Verse

Those who live according to the sinful nature have their minds set on what that nature desires; but those who live in accordance with the Spirit have their minds set on what the Spirit desires. (Romans 8:5)

Goals for Growth

- Realize that a life controlled by the flesh leads to death.
- Learn how to set my mind on the Spirit.
- Commit to putting the flesh to death by walking in the Spirit.

Head Start

I (Todd) have flown countless times in my life, and I'm sure you have too. Yet I bet you've never tried to help the plane off the ground by flapping your arms like a sandhill crane. No amount of flapping will lift that plane into the sky. But could you imagine the pilot asking everybody sitting next to a window to stick out an arm and start flapping?

But that's exactly what we're doing when we try to live the Christian life by our own strength. That's our problem as men. We think our own efforts alone will enable us to soar above our sins and live free from the control of the flesh.

Paul argues that the law of the Spirit has been made available to you. The Holy Spirit will enable you to soar when you cooperate with this new law. It's like the law of gravity or the law of aerodynamics. It exists whether or not you believe in it. But just as you can't overcome gravity unless you actually board a plane, you can't overcome a sinful lifestyle unless you allow the Holy Spirit to control you.

I've come to realize that everything I want to become happens through the power and influence of the Spirit. He alone is the change agent. The Israelites didn't have this ever-present power. They only witnessed the glory of God indirectly as it radiated from Moses, who veiled his face so the people wouldn't see the glory fading away. (See Exodus 34:29-35 and 2 Corinthians 3:13.)

But in Christ, there is no veil! As 2 Corinthians 3:18 says, "We, who with unveiled faces all reflect the Lord's glory, are being transformed into his likeness with ever-increasing glory, which comes from the Lord, who is the Spirit." Did you catch that? The Holy Spirit changes the heart of the man who comes in contact with God through Christ. The Holy Spirit, who dwells within us, will bring about this mystical, unexplainable change in our lives. (See 2 Corinthians 3:16.) But we must submit to His leading. (See Romans 8.) As we learn to be in tune with the Spirit, we will discover how to walk in holiness in this new life God has given us.

Connect with the Word

Read Romans 8.

1. What did Paul say the Holy Spirit has already accomplished in our lives (verses 2-4)?

2. According to verses 4, 5, and 13, what do we need to do for the Spirit to work in our lives?

3. In practical, everyday terms, what does it look like for a man to...

   live according to the Spirit?

set his mind on the Spirit?

4. What are the practical challenges of doing this?

5. What do you think it means to put to death the misdeeds of the body (the sinful flesh) by living in the Spirit (verse 13)? What do you think this looks like in a man's life, practically speaking?

Connect with the Group

Group Opener
Read the group opener aloud and discuss the questions that follow.

When I (Todd) was in college, I worked with Campus Crusade for Christ. We'd venture onto a campus, share the *Four Spiritual Laws* with other college students, and lead them to Christ. Every once in a while I'd run into a believer who wasn't walking with the Lord. He knew the gospel and confessed to being a Christian, but he didn't know how to live it. So I'd pull out a blue booklet with these words emblazoned across it: *Have You Made the Wonderful Discovery of the Spirit-Filled Life?* In most cases the difference between professing faith in Christ and living for Him came down to the person's understanding of what the Holy Spirit can do in a believer's life.

Maybe at this point in the study, you still feel inadequate to live consistently for Christ. "It's just not happening for me," you say. Well, I have good news. Paul's entire argument in Romans will help you understand the role of the Holy Spirit in your life.

Sadly, we are more familiar with daily dependence on our local Starbucks, our cell phones, and our business expense accounts than we are with what it means to depend on the Spirit. Pulling off this Spirit-living takes trust and obedience. It comes down to how intensely we desire to let the Spirit have complete control of our lives. Are you ready for Him to take control?

Discussion Questions

a. To what extent have you attempted to live the Christian life without the power and influence of the Holy Spirit? What evidence supports your response?

b. How can you tell when you are working against the law of the Spirit?

c. What do you think it will take for you to be led by the Holy Spirit? What difference do you think this would make in your life?

d. Romans 8:6-8 describes a man dominated by the flesh and completely overtaken by sin. How do you think it feels to come to a place of helplessness in the face of habitual sin? Describe your own experience of this.

e. According to Romans 8:9-14, what is a man's only remedy for this dilemma? Talk about your own experience of the Spirit's controlling influence in your life.

Standing Strong

From this point on, think of your life as being controlled by the Holy Spirit. What three practical things can you do to stay under the influence of the Holy Spirit every day?

letting God win

Key Verses

One of you will say to me: "Then why does God still blame us? For who resists his will?" But who are you, O man, to talk back to God? "Shall what is formed say to him who formed it, 'Why did you make me like this?' " Does not the potter have the right to make out of the same lump of clay some pottery for noble purposes and some for common use? (Romans 9:19-21)

Goals for Growth

- Believe that God knows what He's doing in my life.
- Adjust any part of my attitude that resists letting God have His way in my life.
- Be more grateful for my salvation and my new life in Christ.

Head Start

A man's most significant battle is often with God Himself over who will control his life. As a man fights for control, the world, the flesh, and the devil gang up against him, betting he won't fully submit himself to God's sovereign control. In fact, everything within a man fights against giving control to God. If the man succumbs to the temptation to retain control, he continues living in darkness and fear. But when he yields to God, the bright, verdant path to godliness and character development opens before him. Which way will he choose?

Remember one thing: the battle against God for control of your life is a battle you will eventually lose. He alone has sovereign control over your life—not you. Practically speaking, if you are going to live a life of faith, set free from the power of sin, you are going to have to settle up with God over who's in control. Like Jacob, every man faces this kind of encounter with God.

Jacob had run from God since the day he deceived his brother for the birthright. After living on the run for more than twenty years, he met God face to face and settled things once and for all:

So Jacob was left alone, and a man wrestled with him till daybreak. When the man saw that he could not overpower him, he touched the socket of Jacob's hip so that his hip was wrenched as he wrestled with the man. Then the man said, "Let me go, for it is daybreak."

But Jacob replied, "I will not let you go unless you bless me."

The man asked him, "What is your name?"

"Jacob," he answered.

Then the man said, "Your name will no longer be Jacob, but Israel, because you have struggled with God and with men and have overcome." (Genesis 32:24-28)

b. What are some of the ways men show their stubbornness toward God?

c. How has Romans 9–11 helped you see that God is sovereign and in charge? What will it take to move that head knowledge into heart-motivated action?

d. When, if ever, have you responded to God with humble submission, accepting His mercy and grace? What does it mean for you to respond this way?

e. In what ways will a humble attitude help you face the challenges you are experiencing at this moment?

f. When did you confess Jesus as Lord of your life (Romans 10:9)? Tell the guys in your group about your experience. (*Suggestion:* If you haven't made this confession yet, why not do it today?)

Standing Strong

In light of the fact that God is the potter and we are the clay, what do you think God is trying to mold out of your life? Be specific and bring the question before the Lord in prayer. What do you think He wants to remove from your life? What do you think He wants to add?

small-group resources

leader tips

What if men aren't doing the Connect with the Word section before our small-group session?

Don't be discouraged. You set the pace. If you are doing the study and regularly referring to it in conversations with your men throughout the week, they will pick up on its importance. Here are some suggestions to motivate the men in your group to do their home Bible study:

- Send out a midweek e-mail in which you share your answer to one of the study questions. This shows them that you are personally committed to and involved in the study.

- Ask the guys to hit "respond to all" on their e-mail program and share one insight from that week's Bible study with the entire group. Encourage them to send it out before the next small-group session.

- Every time you meet, ask each man in the group to share one insight from his home study.

What if men are not showing up for small group?

This might mean they are losing a sin battle and don't want to admit it to the group. Or they might be consumed with other priorities. Or maybe they don't think they're getting anything out of the group. Here are some suggestions for getting the guys back each week:

- Affirm them when they show up, and tell them how much it means to you that they make small group a priority.

- From time to time, ask them to share one reason small group is important to them.
- Regularly call or send out an e-mail the day before you meet to remind them you're looking forward to seeing them.
- Check in with any guy who has missed more than one session and find out what's going on in his life.
- Get some feedback from the men. You may need to adjust your style. Listen and learn.

What if group discussion is not happening?

You are a discussion facilitator. You have to keep guys involved in the discussion or you'll lose them. You can engage a man who isn't sharing by saying, "Chuck, you've been quiet. What do you think about this question or discussion?" You should also be prepared to share your own personal stories that are related to the discussion questions. You'll set the example by the kind of sharing you do.

What if one man is dominating the group time?

You have to deal with it. If you don't, men will stop showing up. No one wants to hear from just one guy all the time. It will quickly kill morale. Meet with the guy in person and privately. Firmly but gently suggest that he allow others more time to talk. Be positive and encouraging, but truthful. You might say, "Bob, I notice how enthusiastic you are about the group and how you're always prepared to share your thoughts with the group. But there are some pretty quiet guys in the group too. Have you noticed? Would you be willing to help me get them involved in speaking up?"

How do I get the guys in my group more involved?

Give them something to do. Ask one guy to bring a snack. Invite another to lead the prayer time (ask in advance). Have a guy sub for you one week as the leader. (Meet with him beforehand to walk through the group program and the time allotments for each segment.) Encourage another guy to lead a subgroup.

What if guys are not being vulnerable during the Standing Strong or prayer times?

You model openness. You set the pace. Honesty breeds honesty. Vulnerability breeds vulnerability. Are you being vulnerable and honest about your own problems and struggles? (This doesn't mean that you have to spill your guts each week or reveal every secret of your life.) Remember, men want an honest, on-their-level leader who strives to walk with God. (Also, as the leader, you need an accountability partner, perhaps another group leader.)

What will we do at the first session?

We encourage you to open by discussing the **Small-Group Covenant** we've included in this resource section. Ask the men to commit to the study, and then discuss how long it will take your group to complete each session. (We suggest 75-90 minute sessions.) Men find it harder to come up with excuses for missing a group session if they have made a covenant to the other men right at the start.

Begin to identify ways certain men can play a more active role in small group. Give away responsibility. You won't feel as burdened, and your men will grow from the experience. Keep in mind that this process can take a few weeks. Challenge men to fulfill one of the group roles identified later in this resource section. If no one steps forward to fill a role, say to one of the men, "George, I've noticed that you are comfortable praying in a group. Would you lead us each week during that time?"

How can we keep the group connected after we finish a study?
Begin talking about starting another Bible study before you finish this eight-week study. (There are several other studies to choose from in the Every Man Bible study series.) Consider having a social time at the conclusion of the study, and encourage the men to invite a friend. This will help create momentum and encourage growth as you launch into another study with your group. There are probably many men in your church or neighborhood who aren't in small groups but would like to be. Be the kind of group that includes others.

As your group grows, consider choosing an apprentice leader who can take half the group into another room for the **Connect with the Group** time. That subgroup can stay together for prayer, or you can reconvene as a large group during that time. You could also meet for discussion as a large group and then break into subgroups for **Standing Strong** and **prayer**.

If your group doubles in size, it might be a perfect opportunity to release your apprentice leader with half the group to start another group. Allow men to pray about this and make a decision as a group. Typically, the relational complexities that come into play when a small group births a new group work themselves out. Allow guys to choose which group they'd like to be a part of. If guys are slow in choosing one group or another, ask them individually to select one of the groups. Take the lead in making this happen.

Look for opportunities for your group to serve in the church or community. Consider a local outreach project or a short-term missions trip. There are literally hundreds of practical ways you can serve the Lord in outreach. Check with your church leaders to learn the needs in your congregation or community. Create some interest by sending out scouts who will return with a report for the group. Serving keeps men from becoming self-focused and ingrown. When you serve as a group, you will grow as a group.

using this study in a large-group format

Many church leaders are looking for biblically based curriculum that can be used in a large-group setting, such as a Sunday-school class, or for small groups within an existing larger men's group. Each of the Every Man Bible studies can be adapted for this purpose. In addition, this curriculum can become a catalyst for churches wishing to launch men's small groups or to build a men's ministry.

Getting Started

Begin by getting the word out to men in your church, inviting them to join you for a men's study based on one of the topics in the Every Man Bible study series. You can place a notice in your church bulletin, have the pastor announce it from the pulpit, or pursue some other means of attracting interest.

Orientation Week

Arrange your room with round tables and chairs. Put approximately six chairs at each table.

Start your session in prayer and introduce your topic with a short but motivational message from any of the scriptures used in the Bible study. Hand out the curriculum and challenge the men to do their homework before each session. During this first session give the men some discussion questions based upon an overview of the material and have them talk things through within their small group around the table.

Just before you wrap things up, have each group select a table host or leader. You can do this by having everyone point at once to the person at their table they feel would best facilitate discussion for future meetings.

Ask those newly elected table leaders to stay after for a few minutes, and offer them an opportunity to be further trained as small-group leaders as they lead discussions throughout the course of the study.

Subsequent Weeks

Begin in prayer. Then give a short message (15-25 minutes) based upon the scripture used for that lesson. Pull out the most motivating topics or points, and strive to make the discussion relevant to the everyday life and world of a typical man. Then leave time for each table to work through the discussion questions listed in the curriculum. Be sure the discussion facilitators at each table close in prayer.

At the end of the eight sessions, you might want to challenge each "table group" to become a small group, inviting them to meet regularly with their new small-group leader and continue building the relationships they've begun.

prayer request record

Date:
Name:
Prayer Request:
Praise:

Date:
Name:
Prayer Request:
Praise:

Date:
Name:
Prayer Request:
Praise:

Date:
Name:
Prayer Request:
Praise:

Date:
Name:
Prayer Request:
Praise:

defining group roles

Group Leader: Leads the lesson and facilitates group discussion.

Apprentice Leader: Assists the leader as needed, which may include leading the lesson.

Refreshment Coordinator: Maintains a list of who will provide refreshments. Calls group members on the list to remind them to bring what they signed up for.

Prayer Warrior: Serves as the contact person for prayer between sessions. Establishes a list of those willing to pray for needs that arise. Maintains the prayer-chain list and activates the chain as needed by calling the first person on the list.

Social Chairman: Plans any desired social events during group sessions or at another scheduled time. Gathers members for planning committees as needed.

small-group roster

Name:
Address:
Phone: E-mail:

Name:
Address:
Phone: E-mail:

Name:
Address:
Phone: E-mail:

Name:
Address:
Phone: E-mail:

Name:
Address:
Phone: E-mail:

Name:
Address:
Phone: E-mail:

spiritual checkup

Your answers to the statements below will help you determine which areas you need to work on in order to grow spiritually. Mark the appropriate letter to the left of each statement. Then make a plan to take one step toward further growth in each area. Don't forget to pray for the Lord's wisdom before you begin. Be honest. Don't be overly critical or rationalize your weaknesses.

Y = Yes
S = Somewhat or Sometimes
N = No

My Spiritual Connection with Other Believers

____ I am developing relationships with Christian friends.

____ I have joined a small group.

____ I am dealing with conflict in a biblical manner.

____ I have become more loving and forgiving than I was a year ago.

____ I am a loving and devoted husband and father.

My Spiritual Growth

____ I have committed to daily Bible reading and prayer.

____ I am journaling on a regular basis, recording my spiritual growth.

___ I am growing spiritually by studying the Bible with others.

___ I am honoring God in my finances and personal giving.

___ I am filled with joy and gratitude for my life, even during trials.

___ I respond to challenges with peace and faith instead of anxiety and anger.

___ I avoid addictive behaviors (excessive drinking, overeating, watching too much TV, etc.).

Serving Christ and Others

___ I am in the process of discovering my spiritual gifts and talents.

___ I am involved in ministry in my church.

___ I have taken on a role or responsibility in my small group.

___ I am committed to helping someone else grow in his spiritual walk.

Sharing Christ with Others

___ I care about and am praying for those around me who are unbelievers.

___ I share my experience of coming to know Christ with others.

___ I invite others to join me in this group or for weekend worship services.

___ I am praying for others to come to Christ and am seeing this happen.

___ I do what I can to show kindness to people who don't know Christ.

Surrendering My Life for Growth

___ I attend church services weekly.

___ I pray for others to know Christ, and I seek to fulfill the Great Commission.

___ I regularly worship God through prayer, praise, and music, both at church and at home.

___ I care for my body through exercise, nutrition, and rest.

___ I am concerned about using my energy to serve God's purposes instead of my own.

My Identity in the Lord

___ I see myself as a beloved son of God, one whom God loves regardless of my sin.

___ I can come to God in all of my humanity and know that He accepts me completely. When I fail, I willingly run to God for forgiveness.

___ I experience Jesus as an encouraging Friend and Lord each moment of the day.

___ I have an abiding sense that God is on my side. I am aware of His gracious presence with me throughout the day.

___ During moments of beauty, grace, and human connection, I lift up praise and thanks to God.

___ I believe that using my talents to their fullest pleases the Lord.

___ I experience God's love for me in powerful ways.

small-group covenant

As a committed group member, I agree to the following:*

- **Regular Attendance.** I will attend group sessions on time and let everyone know in advance if I can't make it.
- **Group Safety.** I will help create a safe, encouraging environment where men can share their thoughts and feelings without fear of embarrassment or rejection. I will not judge other guys or attempt to fix their problems.
- **Confidentiality.** I will always keep to myself everything that is shared in the group.
- **Acceptance.** I will respect different opinions or beliefs and let Scripture be the teacher.
- **Accountability.** I will make myself accountable to the other group members for the personal goals I share.
- **Friendliness.** I will look for those around me who might join the group and explore their faith with other men.
- **Ownership.** I will prayerfully consider taking on a specific role within the group as the opportunity arises.
- **Spiritual Growth.** I will commit to establishing a daily quiet time with God, which includes doing the homework for this study. I will share with the group the progress I make and the struggles I experience as I seek to grow spiritually.

Signed: _____ Date: _____

---

*   *Permission is given to photocopy and distribute this form to each man in your group. Review this covenant quarterly or as needed.*

about the authors

STEPHEN ARTERBURN is coauthor of the best-selling Every Man series. He is also founder and chairman of New Life Clinics, host of the daily *New Life Live!* national radio program, and creator of the Women of Faith conferences. A nationally known speaker and licensed minister, Stephen has authored more than forty books. He lives with his family in Laguna Beach, California.

KENNY LUCK is president and founder of Every Man Ministries, coauthor of *Every Man, God's Man* and its companion workbook, and coauthor of the Every Man Bible studies. He is the area leader for men's ministry and teaches a men's interactive Bible study at Saddleback Church in Lake Forest, California. He and his wife, Chrissy, have three children and reside in Trabuco Canyon, California.

TODD WENDORFF is a graduate of University of California, Berkeley, and holds a ThM from Talbot School of Theology. He serves as a teaching pastor at King's Harbor Church in Redondo Beach and is an adjunct professor at Biola University. He is an author of the Doing Life Together Bible study series. Todd and his wife, Denise, live with their three children in Rolling Hills Estates, California.

start a bible study
and connect with others
who want to be God's man.

Every Man Bible Studies are designed to help you discover, own, and build on convictions grounded in God's word.

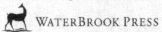

every man's battle workshops

from New Life Ministries

new Life Ministries receives hundreds of calls every month from Christian men who are struggling to stay pure in the midst of daily challenges to their sexual integrity and from pastors who are looking for guidance in how to keep fragile marriages from falling apart all around them.

As part of our commitment to equip individuals to win these battles, New Life Ministries has developed biblically based workshops directly geared to answer these needs. These workshops are held several times per year around the country.

- Our workshops **for men** are structured to equip men with the tools necessary to maintain sexual integrity and enjoy healthy, productive relationships.

- Our workshops **for church leaders** are targeted to help pastors and men's ministry leaders develop programs to help families being attacked by this destructive addiction.

Some comments from previous workshop attendees:

"An awesome, life-changing experience. Awesome teaching, teacher, content and program." —DAVE

"God has truly worked a great work in me since the EMB workshop. I am fully confident that with God's help, I will be restored in my ministry position. Thank you for your concern. I realize that this is a battle, but I now have the weapons of warfare as mentioned in Ephesians 6:10, and I am using them to gain victory!" —KEN

"It's great to have a workshop you can confidently recommend to anyone without hesitation, knowing that it is truly life changing. Your labors are not in vain!" —DR. BRAD STENBERG, Pasadena, CA

If sexual temptation is threatening your marriage or your church, please call **1-800-NEW-LIFE** to speak with one of our specialists.

Printed in the United States
by Baker & Taylor Publisher Services